The Core 7

Building and Mastering Your Best You

MICHEL MCKENZIE

This book is dedicated to my loving mother and father, Marcia and Ranell McKenzie. Th*ank you for all your love and support. Everything I am is a testament to everything you have done for me.*

MICHEL MCKENZIE

Copyright and Intellectual Property Owner © Michel McKenzie

Copyright 2016© Michel McKenzie. All rights reserved. No part of this book may be reproduced in any form or by any electronic or mechanical means, including information storage and retrieval systems, without permission in writing from the publisher, except by a reviewer, who may quote brief passages in a review.

Book Written by: Michel McKenzie

Publisher Name: Michel McKenzie

Contact Name: Michel McKenzie

Contact Email: dreamingrealities1@gmail.com

ISBN-13: 978-0-9949273-2-3

Table of Contents

THE LESS PREFERRED ROAD 5
ARE YOU A DREAMER? 10
VALIDATION 16
21-QUESTION ASSESSMENT 20
THE CORE 7 27
GOAL SETTING: UTILIZING THE CORE 7 42
PLAN OF ACTION 47
TAKE MY ADVICE 54
MY FINAL THOUGHTS 59

THE LESS PREFERRED ROAD

Imagine with me for a moment that you are travelling down a road. This road just like any other road has its own unique bumps and potholes but despite those imperfections the scenery travelling down this road is ab-solutely beautiful. Not only is the scenery beautiful you also get the op-portunity to share it with the people that you love. You feel accepted and validated because of what you see and who you are with but there is just one problem; the road that you are travelling on does not bring you to your required destination. It may possibly bring you somewhere interest-ing however this particular road wasn't designed to take you to where you are supposed to arrive. Perhaps this seems a bit wasteful because you may ask yourself the question, *why would I travel down a road that doesn't take me to where I am supposed to be going*? That is the most logical question you could ask yourself and by right you should be able to come up with a reasonable, sensible answer. Why drive east when my destination is west, or why drive north when my destination is south?

Now equate this road to be the path in life that you are supposed to travel on. Despite the beautiful scenery, flock of family and friends, it all is pointless and doesn't make logical sense to travel on regardless of the happiness and joy it seemingly may bring. So my question now is why do most people choose this road to travel on? Could it be that the road has just not yet been discovered to be the wrong one or could one be travelling so fast they become out of control? Both are great possibilities and we could conclude at either one of them. Don't waste your time, energy and resources going through life without a focused destination in mind. Life is a gift and it would surely be wasteful if we just cruised through it with no concrete destination in mind. Are you travelling down the road that leads to your dreams and a better you, or are you driving aimlessly down the road that takes you to a destination you don't know.

Living out your dreams may take you down a road that may not be full of all your desired family and friends at times, however living out your dream will take you down a road that will lead you to your happiness, peace and abundance. You'll find that everything you truly need and ap-preciate will be on this path.

Your happiness is subjective to your perspective and your sufferings are subjective to your desires, you can only be happy based on how you view life or what you think matters. Riches do not bring happiness. They only amplify happiness if it is already there and you will always feel suffering as long as your desires outweigh your capability to bring those desires to a reality.

Are you willing to travel the road that is less preferred? It may not come with all of your friends and family that you envisioned being there and it may not have the exact scenery you always imagined it would have, but can you be okay with that? Your life will never seem to have a concrete purpose until you take the nearest exist sign and get onto this road. Would you be willing to take a path that may go against the grain, through some dark tunnels and winding turns but ultimately to your ideal destination? When you arrive at this des-tination you will not only be living out your purpose but you will also be the best version of yourself. Often times when my family or friends and I decide to travel, we make sure we have our G.P.S (Global

Positioning System) with us. When you are travelling to an un-known destination it is so important that you have something or someone with you that knows where to go. Usually G.P.S systems will come with an electronic voice that is designed to guide you every step of the way.

Sometimes while driving to my desired destination the G.P.S will take me into some unfamiliar territory, however I do not allow myself to get bothered by what I do not understand because I know that I just need to keep on driv-ing until the G.P.S tells me that I have arrived at my destination. It is not really about where I am that truly matters if I know exactly where I'm going and how to get there. As simple as using a G.P.S may sound, countless people would rather put their trust into a machine rather than into themselves. The reality is many people decide to listen to the voices around them instead of listen-ing to themselves. They are being misguided by people who truly do not understand them or their destination. In this book, I want to share with you some valuable information that will help you drive down the less preferred road. The less preferred road cannot be driven on like any other road. Your destiny is found on this road, it is yours to take or leave. You have the choice to either go through the pain of failure or the pain of success.

"Your happiness is subjective to your perspective and your sufferings are subjective to your desires, you can only be happy based on how you view life or what you think matters. Riches do not bring happiness. They only amplify happiness if it is already there and you will always feel suffering as long as your desires outweigh your capability to bring those desires to a reality."

ARE YOU A DREAMER?

Close your eyes for a moment and imagine accomplishing your greatest dream. This is the dream that you have been waiting for and it is finally a part of your reality. I believe dreams were designed to come true and that we were all born to live a life of happiness and abundance. Due to corrup-tion and selfish desires however, we experience a great imbalance upon the earth which makes it significantly more difficult to believe in ourselves. Many folks grew up with the ideology that dreams are not meant to be real and as a result this burning desire for happiness and fruitfulness became overlooked and caged in their hearts. Let me take you back to your child-hood for a brief moment. This is the time when your dreams were not only part of your everyday life but they seemed possible and achievable. It is my belief that we were all born to be dreamers. As a matter of fact our dreams contribute to our overall wholeness as human beings.

In other words, our fulfilled dreams contribute to the piece of the puzzle that completes our life experience. When we are conscious of our thoughts we "dream realities" and although we are young the intuition to have a life of abundance can easily be recognized. No child dreams of being anything but above average! Despite our initial circumstances and family backgrounds our dreams are all hopeful and optimistic.

From the most privileged to the least privileged child in the world, there is an uncontrollable desire to belong and contribute to the world. Ultimately we were born and designed to dream. As we transition from childhood to adolescence and then to adulthood, we begin to experience life on a far more complex level than any of us would ever imagine. Our situations become and the overall pressure of life becomes overwhelming. There are deadlines to meet, bills to pay and mouths to feed.

Our dreams slowly start slipping away and the new driving force of life is to simply accomplish anything of significant worth. What happened to the dreamer? What happened to the voice and thoughts of abundance? All of the hopes you once had for yourself are silenced. Yet from time to time you are reminded of all your aspirations and true desires. Abundance, happiness and peace lay dormant inside you due to the overwhelming nature of life and soon the voice of fear and doubt became louder than the voice of your dreams. Your dreams however, deserve to live and there is a place for them in this world. You deserve to be that somebody you've always imagined yourself to be.

You deserve that promotion or that dream house; maybe that dream trip, and that recognition you've always felt you deserved! These are all yours to attain!

Two of the main reasons dreams do not become part of our reality is because 1) we get caught up in the fears and doubts leading us to be-lieve that our dreams are not meant for us to achieve. 2) We do not **create a plan and set goals** towards our dreams leaving them to float away. We live in a world today where the idea of "fine living" has been heavily ingrained into our fast paced culture. The world has adopted a "want it now" mentality and as a result, there has been added pressure and stress to our society. More people are depressed, confused, and ungrateful toward their current life because of this grand desire to be successful. Although the world will always adapt new philosophies and mindsets the desire for success and fulfillment will never change. It can be a deadly choice to adapt a mindset without the proper information to go along with it. The consequences of this will result in unintentionally setting ourselves up for a sub-par life.

More and more people today are chasing an idea of a reality they have no way of truly attaining. If you ask most people whether they want to be successful in life, the answer would be an obvious 'yes!'. However, if you proceeded to ask them how they would go about it, the answer might be significantly less enthusiastic and they may or may not have a clear plan to follow.

The issue is clearly not the desire but rather the steps one takes to achieving those desires. Most people, if not all, can see the finish line but cannot see the path. The truth is that there is in fact no real path to see rather, it is your job to cre-ate one. Your path is created by your strategy and your understanding of the little steps you have to take in order to achieve success. The road of purpose is filled with walls and barriers and the only way to see what is on the other side is to plan, have faith in yourself and execute those plans by climbing over the walls and the barriers one at a time. It should be no secret that in order for a person to live a successful, fulfilling life they must set realistic goals and meet those goals.

Dreams and projects do not just happen with excellence unless you in-tentionally prepare yourself for them. Look at it this way, your dreams are your ultimate destination and the goals you make for yourself become the G.P.S route that will take you there. It is more than just writing a few ideas down on paper with a deadline, but in fact strategically mapping out your plan of action so that you have a greater, more probable chance of achiev-ing success. Everyone was born to be successful. The difference between successful people and non-successful people is that successful people in-tentionally do things to make themselves successful and keep themselves there. However, it shouldn't disregard the fact that some people's path to success will be harder than others.

I want you to understand that it is more than necessary to set goals.

Your goals give you a purpose for waking up each morning. It is that extra push when you feel like you cannot go on. It is that motivation to keep you working hard even when the end result isn't clear. It is that unquenchable fire you will learn to kindle and it will be the reason you can inspire some-one else to keep reaching for their dreams. Life will always be so much more fulfilling when you have something to work towards and let me em-phasize the word *work* because that's exactly what it will take for you to separate yourself from the rest. Dreams were designed to come true and you can make yours happen.

VALIDATION

You will not get to your destination in life until you travel your distinct road. When you finally get positioned on this path it is no longer about 'keeping up' or doing anything to appease the people around you. It will be completely about just doing what needs to be done in order to move your life forward. Your train of thought will include statements such as, *what is going to work for me?* and *What am I willing to change or sacrifice?* You are not validated by what you have or what you can do. You are validated based upon who you are and what you know you are capable of doing. That is all you need! When you live to please people the only person that will end up being unsatisfied is yourself. You were not born to impress you were born to impact! How can you use what you have to impact this world posi-tively?

When I'm driving on the highway from time to time, I will come across that one driver that is speeding and constantly switching lanes. This is quite a common occurrence and it is fair to question the driver's actions. Most people may assume the driver is either drunk or crazy. Pertaining to our lives, we too are often speeding and switching lanes when unnecessary. The phrase 'stay in your lane' is often mentioned however, I have discovered that applying this phrase to oneself can be more difficult and pressuring than it may seem to appear. How can one stay in their lane of life when they do not even understand what lane they are in to begin with?

When you constantly switch lanes in your life you will begin to travel on roads that were never intended for you to travel on and in turn get frustrated when you do not see the results you expected to see. When you are constantly chasing the validation of people, your life and its events will mimic that of a seemingly crazy, drunk driver. It would appear as if you have no clear destination or focus. You will make irrational choices and not see them through and you will always be moving at different speeds. Now, I never said the seemingly crazy, drunk driver was actually even drunk or never had a destination in mind. Rather, it would just appear as if they didn't. How can you get the support you need or access to the right resources to change your life and build your dreams when you don't seem to be secure in yourself? When you are living for others you will become confused with who you want to be and what you are allowing yourself to become.

You will be amazed at the power and freedom you feel and experience when you begin to allow yourself to just exhale and be. Your goals and dreams matter and how you feel matters as well. We all have dreams, goals and feelings so why should you sacrifice yours at the expense of someone else's? Life can put us into positions where we have to make some tough decisions but that doesn't mean our dreams die because of the few difficult situations that life presents. Compromising your integrity is like opening up a black hole into your life. You will be in relationships you don't want to be in, be a part of movements you have no real interest in, and you will sacrifice the important people and treasures in your life to temporarily satisfy the people around you. We have the power to eliminate excess stress, problems and heartache out of our lives. Chasing false validation will eventually dictate to you some things that never had to be heard, visualized and experienced. Your past is what made you who you currently are however your future is dependent on who you are growing to be. Your happiness, peace of mind, joy and feeling of fulfillment will be awakened once you make the decision to do what's best for you.

"Compromising your integrity is like opening up a black hole into your life. You will be in relationships you don't want to be in, be a part of movements you have no real interest in, and you will sacrifice the important people and treasures in your life to temporarily satisfy the people around you."

21-QUESTION ASSESSMENT

This 21-question assessment will be able to help pinpoint your areas of strength and weakness. Each question refers to a specific category which represents one of the 7 aspects of the CORE 7. All 21 questions are worth a maximum of 10 points and a minimum of 0 each. At the end of the as-sessment you will add up each individual category and then total your score.

Yes or no questions will be indicated with (*)

If you indicate "No" where there is an (*) please mark 'No' wherever else you see an (*)

Score

Do I have a career currently?   (C)
0 = no, 10 = yes
_____

How good a life do I want to life?   (BD)
0 = It doesn't matter 10 = The best life I can possibly have

_____

Is money my biggest motivation?   (FS)
0 = that is all I think about, 10 = Not at all _____

How well do I know myself?   (R)
0= I don't know myself at all, 10= I know everything there is to know about me _____

Has my career been killing my ultimate dreams, hopes and goals? (C)
0= It has completely been, 10=not at all _____

Do I have support?   (F)
0 = none at all, 10 = more than enough _____

Am I self-conscious of my appearance?   (PE)
0 = it is the most important thing to me, 10 = not at all,

_____

How much am I holding on to painful past experiences (M)
0 = I don't know how to let go, 10 = I've let them all go

_____

Am I dependent on people? (R)

0 = I can't live without them 10 = not at all,

_____

How much does money control my happiness? (FS)

0 = I can't be happy without it, 10 = I don't need it to be happy

_____

Am I happy with my current situation pertaining to my career? (Compensation, hours, security, growth potential, benefits, loca-tion and working environment) (C)

0 = I'm completely not happy, 10 = I'm completely happy.

_____

Have I forgiven those that have hurt me? (R)

0= They don't deserve it, 10 = Yes I have whole heartedly

_____

How much do I follow what I believe? (BD)

0 = I don't at all, 10 = I completely follow everything

_____

How much does my family mean to me? (F)
0 = it means nothing to me, 10= it means everything to me

_____

Have I been letting a negative mindset affect my behavior?
(M) 0 = completely, 10=not at all_____

Am I limiting myself because of fear? (BD)
0 =it has crippled my life, 10 =fear has no hold over me

_____

How much does a healthy lifestyle mean to me? (PE)
0 = I don't care to live healthy, 10= it means everything to me

_____

Do I want my own family? (F)
0 = all I need is myself, 10= of course I want one!

_____

THE CORE 7

Am I driven by my emotions? (PE)
0 = completely, 10=never _____

How much does money mean to me? (C)
0 = it means the world to me, 10= I do not care for it at all

_____

Am I a positive or negative thinker? (M)
0 = negative, 10 = positive _____

Now tally up your score based on color:
Family (F)
Beliefs and Desires (BD)
Mindset (M)
Physical and Emotional Wellbeing (PE)
Career (C)
Financial Security (FS)
Relationships ®
Total points= _____

(21 questions=210 possible points)

For each category:

If you have scored **0-12** in any category it means you need to pay special at-tention to this specific area

If you have scored **13-21** in any category it means that this area needs work but is not of any serious concern.

If you scored **22-30** in any category it means you are doing exception-ally well in this area.

For your overall score

If you have scored **0-71** you should be very concerned with your overall well-being. A score in this range means you that you lack a balanced life. I would advise you to get a life coach or even speak to a therapist or psy-chologist. You're going to need to get someone in your corner to help you make the changes necessary to move forward.

If you have scored **72-141** you are not in great risk however you need to make sure you pay attention to the areas where you scored low and inten-tionally work towards making them better. Maybe a life coach, therapist or psychologist could help you iron out the areas that are hindering you from making progress.

If you have scored **142-210** you are on the right track! Somehow you find a way to make things work for your overall peace, purpose and abundance.

THE CORE 7

Most people say *I want my life to be better* yet they are unable to articulate why. They just know life isn't what they want it to be and that's as far as it goes. Wanting your life to be better is great however it has to be understood that it is a lot more complex than this general statement. Life is compiled with so many different obstacles and priorities that it may be too overwhelming to really zone in on the areas that one wishes to see improvement. There are 7 major areas of focus that make up our complete balance to life. Through these major areas we uncover who we are and form our understanding of life. It is very important that we keep these areas completely balanced at all times in order to be stable, happy and whole. From birth, the first thing we do as babies is cleave to our mothers. It is where we initially feel safe and through this experience we get our first hand importance of **family**

There is a famous quote that says 'it takes a village to raise a child' and this is a definite truth. From childhood, the first place that we look for support is from our family. Our family was designed to be our main sup-port system and backbone behind our ambitions and dreams.

It is also through family or lack of family that determines our beliefs. Unfortunately not everyone has the privilege of being raised

in what we would call the traditional, nuclear family however, just like the quote says, it takes a village to raise a child. It is through schools, religious gatherings, community oriented programs and support groups where chil-dren also have the opportunity to develop their rudimentary beliefs and their support system. Once our idea of family is established our **beliefs and desires** will begin to take form.

It is our beliefs that govern our moral decisions and overall outlook on life. Where there are no beliefs there will also be no concrete foun-dation. They are the laws that are written on our heart that give us hope, faith and purpose. Through our beliefs and support we will develop our desires and ambition towards life. A person who has a strong sup-port system and a set of positive beliefs is more likely to have positive desires towards life. It is your desires that govern your overall morale but it is your beliefs that set the tone for your desires. This is only just the beginning of where the "balancing act" will begin. An understand-ing of desires will birth the beginning of pursuing purpose which leads us to our third factor, our **mindset**. Our beliefs and desires form our mindset.

As our mindset develops it begins to determine the consistency of our beliefs, desires and emotions. Every thought about ourselves and the world we live in stems from the health of our mindset. If you think positively then you will have a positive outlook towards yourself and the world. The same understanding can be applied to a negative mindset. It is through your mindset that you will allow yourself to make things hap-pen. You have to give yourself permission. Indecisiveness flows from a divided mindset and being indecisive is not a quality a winner possesses. Your mind is your president. It makes all the decisions and governs your every move. It is important that we take great caution in what we allow to enter and influence such an important part of our being. We are most conscious of our **physical and emotional well-being** than any other component of who we are. The truth is we just cannot hide who we are and how we feel from ourselves. The disease to our physical prosperity is emotional insecurity which ultimately breeds a lack of self-confidence.

It affects every area of our lives and this one area can single handedly destroy all of our beliefs and desires while slowly eating away at our mind-set. A healthy mindset towards our physical and emotional well-being is the key for positive thinking and positive living. It will help motivate your beliefs, raise your overall morale and help you stay consistent with your mindset. Everything I have covered so far has led us to our fifth factor, our **career**.

Our choices create the path to our destiny. When we do not pursue our heart's desire for our life we fail at giving ourselves a fair opportunity to live in purpose, abundance and wholeness. Our career is not just a "money grab" but a strategic place where your heart is supposed to be able to manifest our dreams, goals and desires. When there is a positive balance between our beliefs, desires, family, mindset and our physical and emotional well-being it will then position us towards our career. What we were put on this earth to do should align harmoniously with our career. **Financial security** is the underlying theme of our society. Our biological clock never stops ticking and the uncertainties of the future never seem to quiet themselves. We wonder if we will have enough money to live our dreams and still take care of our realities at the same time. There is a silent pressure to attain wealth and to maintain it throughout the course of our lives. It is possible to plan and position ourselves financially for the future however that does not exclude the fact that unfortunate, unforeseen circumstances have the power to change that. When we are pursuing our purpose the financial increase for prosperity will come with it. The only time finances will become a burden is when you are out of synch with your purpose.

So far we have looked into six key areas of our life. We have taken our life, created a blueprint and **relationships** represent the last key that needs to be added to it. Relationships are a combination of everything discussed so far that will create them. Relationships are vital to our life existence because all it takes is one bad relationship to destroy every component that I has been discoursed.

Every relationship we are in whether it is with a friend, family member or significant other is supposed to contribute to our wholeness. We were not created to be destroyed by the people around us. Every relationship in our lives must hold positive value. If a relationship causes you to devalue any of the 6 keys mentioned above, it is a relationship not worth having. Time is something we can never govern. We do not have any input in-regards to the length of our life which is why there is absolutely no time to waste on unproductive, unfruitful relationships.

With these 7 factors combined, The CORE 7 is created. It is who we are, why we are and where we're going. When each factor is properly implemented, healthy and maintained success will have an open avenue to flow from. When you set goals and take proper action through these seven fundamentals you will get results. The CORE 7 is your foundation to holistic living and success.

Family

Ask yourself:

How much does my family mean to me?

Am I being the best I can be for my family?

Do I have support?

Do I want my own family?

Having family is so important to our success and our survival. We were born with an ingrained desire to want to have a family. There would be no life without a family. When you look at the world today people have their own blood related family or another group of people they ascribe to be family.

Family can have a positive or negative effect on us. It is the place where we are supposed to gain our confidence and our desires for life. Every per-son in this world is a part of a family whether that's a support group or even a gang we will always cling to where we can find acceptance. With this un-derstanding it is very important that we cherish and appreciate our families.

Beliefs/ Desires

Ask yourself:

How much do I follow what I believe?

Who or what has made the biggest influence on my beliefs? How good a life do I want to life?

Am I limiting myself because of fear?

Your beliefs and desires are the core to your character and your attitude towards life. Our pursuit of life will be always be fueled by our beliefs and desires. Our beliefs shape our desires and our desires shape our dreams. This is the part of us that creates a yearning to see our dreams come to pass. They are woven so tightly together that what happens to one will directly affect the other. What you believe and what you desire creates the foundation to your mindset and as we know now it is our mindset that determines our physical and emotional well-being. Everything is intricately put together and your beliefs and desires cre-ate your heartbeat to life. If you do not desire anything you won't have any motivation for living and if you have no beliefs you will have no principles to live by. You need to firstly believe in who you are and what you can do because by doing this you allow yourself to give your best to the world. Challenge yourself to be true to what you believe and intentional with pursuing your desires. It will help you have a better handle over life.

Mindset

Ask yourself:

Where did I get my current mindset from? Am I a positive or negative thinker?

Have I been letting a negative mindset rule my behavior?
How much am I holding on to painful past experiences?

Your state of mind will have everything to do with how you live and approach life. Life does not begin to happen because of the actions you make but rather the thoughts you think first. It is very simple; if you do not think it then you will not do it. People fail to even recognize were there mindsets come from and as a result they are trapped living subpar lives because of negative, low level thinking. Having a negative mindset will be the cancer to your purpose for living. If you do not have the mindset to be happy or successful, do not expect people to have that opinion of you. The past is the past and it can only dictate your future if you choose to let it. Any actions you make in this life are essentially the choices you make and nothing happens without choices. Choose to be forgiving, happy and positive because by doing so you will make the choice to have a healthy mind and a re-warding life.

Physical/Emotional Well-being

Ask yourself:

How much does a healthy lifestyle mean to me?

Am I self-conscious of my appearance?

Am I driven by my negative emotions?

Do I worry about things that are out of my control?

When you are physically healthy and emotionally stable you are able to live life to its fullest capacity. Your physical and emotional well-being will be key contributors to your mindset. If you are physically unhappy you will also be emotionally unhappy. In essence, whatever you do physically will affect how you feel and act emotionally. Your mind is dependent on these areas to function in a harmonious, united and positive manner. Nobody other than yourself can fix this area of your life and it will take an intentional effort. When you are emotionally happy and motivated you will also be physically motivated.

A balanced life will result in a balanced physical and emotional well-being.

Career

Ask yourself:

Do I have a career currently?

How satisfied am I with my current career?

How happy am I with my current situation pertaining to my ca-reer? (compensation, hours, security, growth potential, benefits, location and working environment)

Has my career been killing my ultimate dreams, hopes and goals?

You can easily be satisfied with your career but still not know what you want to achieve from it. Your career should not be burdensome it should be purposeful. Your career is a part of the legacy you will leave on earth and it will be in the majority of the chapters of your life. It should never simply be about paying bills because we were not born to just survive but to thrive and achieve all that life has to offer.

Financial Security

Ask yourself:

How much does money mean to me?

Is money my biggest motivation or my biggest stressor? How much does money control my happiness?

How much money do I desire to earn?

Money is a huge part of life. Without a "financial flow" we cannot build a life that is abundant and whole. Money is not to be cherished but to be looked at as just a tool that is needed for survival. When we die we cannot take our money to the grave with us as it has no value there. There is also no hierarchy because it is a place where every person becomes equal regardless of how much money they made. With that being said, money is not something you shouldn't want to attain but rather your life value should not be based on your bank account statement. When you can be internally happy, the money you acquire will begin to serve its true purpose. Remember money is not a soul mate and it doesn't have friends or favourites. It is only a tool needed for our survival.

Relationships

Ask yourself:

How well do I know myself?

Am I at a place of balance in my life?

Am I dependent on people?

Have I forgiven those that have hurt me?

The only way to whole heartedly enjoy a relationship with someone whether it be a friend or significant other is to whole heartedly enjoy yourself. We are supposed to contribute to a person's happiness and not be the one who debilitates them emotionally. When it comes to relation-ships the worst thing you can do to yourself is to engage in a relationship without truly knowing and understanding yourself. This will be damaging and it will make the relationship with the other person less valuable because you will not know what you truly bring to the table. Every person that we allow to connect with us should serve a purpose in our lives and I do not say that with any selfish back lining. When you know yourself you can add value to a person's life and appreciate them for who they are. When you do not understand and appreciate yourself first, you are put in a posi-tion to be dependent on others. Many people live their lives today on the backs of other people. They are emotionally paralyzed and they con-stantly seek attention and validation from the people around them. This is toxic because you will eventually become a burden to the people you are around. Every relationship you have with people should be a blessing and not a burden.

GOAL SETTING: UTILIZING THE CORE 7

When you can analyze your life and line it up with the CORE 7 you will see how valuable and powerful it can be. You had all the answers. The issue was just organizing how they could fit into your life. With these core essentials you will be able to lock in on your areas of change. After understanding the CORE 7 the next step is to set goals. Be intentional in your approach to setting realistic, life-changing goals. Your goal setting tool should be fairly simple and easy to follow.

Please consider the following when setting goals:

Create each goal as a positive affirmation – it is important that you only express your goals positively. For example instead of saying, that you want to lose weight to become skinny, you can positively say *"my goal is to eat healthier, and routinely exercise so that I can lose 40 pounds to be at a healthy weight."* Positive affirmations feed your motivation. The more positive you feel about what you are doing the more drive you will have to see to it that it gets done.

Be intentional: Set goals by putting in dates and times and progress checks so that you can accurately measure your achievement. If you do this, you'll know exactly when and how you've achieved your goal and in the process this will help you stay motivated.

Prioritize your goals: This is probably the most crucial and important step to remember when creating goals. Everything hinges on your capa-bility to accurately set the right goals. You can possibly have great goals but if there are too many goals or if you're trying to do too many things at once you're setting yourself up for failure. Your goals need to be organized so that you can accomplish a lot more.

Write your goals down – This should go without saying but unfortu-nately often times people have this grand idea that they will somehow be able to remember everything. This may be true, but in life we can have so many other things to think about that often times our goals will not be at the forefront of our minds. By writing your goals down, you have a few less things to think and worry about. Being able to visually see things will help you stay organized and motivated. Sometimes we will not know how much progress we have made until we can visually see it in front of us. It should be organized in a way where you can see the task and the deadlines.

Set realistic goals – It's important to set goals that you can actually achieve. If you set goals that are too hard or seemingly unattainable you set your-self up for challenges and obstacles you're not mentally prepared to face. Your goal shouldn't aim at becoming a millionaire in one year if you have no job, no income, no resources and no plan. A goal can be to become a millionaire, however what are some practical goals to have in place to see to it that your ultimate goal can be achieved? Set goals that you wholeheartedly believe in.

Set "your" goals: The worst decision you can make in goal-setting is setting your parents' goals or your peers' goals or even your co-workers' goals. The real question that matters is what do *you* want to achieve? Silence the voices around you and listen to your-self. *"What do I really want to accomplish?" "What will take me to the next level in abundant living?"* Whether you realize it or not you will always know and under-stand yourself the most. That being said you know what's really important to you and it is up to you to make it happen.

Your friends and family will try and point you in the direction that they think you should go out of love and concern, however they usually do this out of ignorance of your own desires and ambitions.

After considering the latter, you must thoroughly write out your goal and the purpose for your goal so that when you look at your goal chart you will have a constant reminder of why you are doing what you're doing. This should be written right above the chart and should be kept together. This should be an expression of your heart written on paper so make sure you make this as genuine and thoughtful as possible.

My goal is:

_____

The purpose for my goal is:

_____

Now we get to thoughtfully plot out our vision for how we want our goals to transpire. You now have written down your goal honestly and realis-tically so ask yourself how far along do you want to be after 1 week, 1 month, 3 months, 6 months, 9 months and 1 year. Three month intervals should give you an opportunity to properly gauge your progress and possi-bly make adjustments if necessary. Close your eyes and visually see where you want to be after each marker before writing anything down.

PLAN OF ACTION

It is time to make a plan of action. I know there are many ways you can go about this however, it will be most fruitful if we only create a plan of action after each desired marker is met. Create a plan of action for your first week and only after that first week is done should you sit down and strategize for the next marker. This will help you stay precise, organized and consistently engaged throughout the whole process. After a deadline is met it will be much easier to review your current progress and troubleshoot any difficulties you have had to make it easier and more efficient for yourself. After you have successfully passed a few markers you can review and compare your plans of action for each deadline to start connecting the dots to your journey.

You should always review your purpose for your goal and make sure that through each deadline you are staying true to it. A plan of action is self-explanatory. It is a strategy designed to move forward and conquer each stage set out before you. It is also your list of positive affirmations.

THE CORE 7

This is personally my favorite part of the goal setting process because this is where new beginnings are born and a new path on the road to destiny can be carved out!

There are no secrets and there are no tricks to this. If anyone tries to make it seem as if there are, they are simply trying to take advantage of your misunderstanding. Imagine momentarily that you are playing chess. You know the capabilities of all the pieces that you have on your side and it is up to you to utilize those pieces to make strategic moves to counter the opposing players move. Consider that it is your turn to make a move. Do you just pick up a pieces and move it or do you methodically look at all your options and consider your opponents reaction to your possible moves before you actually make a decision? When two good chess players sit down to play this calculated game, none of their moves happen by chance. Each move is thoroughly thought through and every option and counter move is heavily considered before any move is made. This game can go on for one hour, 12 hours and depending on who is playing one game can even last up to a few days. This part of the process should be the most exciting but also the most realistic and thoughtful.

Let us go through each part of the diagram so you can get a clear under-standing as to how you can utilize this great tool.

The Purpose of this plan is to:

Purpose: Right above this diagram, you may have noticed that there is a section to write out your purpose. By this particular point your goal should already be understood and thought through. By going through the goal section you have already written down the purpose for your goal. It is important that you write it down again so that you can re-affirm what has already been established. Additionally, through your strategic thinking process of your plan in action certain aspects of your purpose may change and this should be noted so that you can see where and how you changed your thinking.

Objective: Objective and purpose may seem one in the same but they both serve different purposes. In your purpose you are stating the reason for why you're doing this which is just your general affirmation. In your objective you are zoning in on a specific task and the objective is high-lighting that task. For example, *"my objective is to complete 40 hours of research, my purpose is to hold seminars based off of the information I gathered through my research."*

If your deadline is a week, what will be the objective for that week? Your objective should change as you meet new deadlines because you will be changing the specific area of focus.

Strategy: This will be the most important piece of the puzzle. If your strategy is not sufficient, your chances of completing your objective will be improbable. Use the chess example as you sit down and thoroughly create this game plan. It will help if you have 1 or 2 trusted individuals to help bounce ideas off of. Based on your objective what will your potential obstacles be? How will you avoid setbacks? How will you attack this objective and what is the smartest way to go about it? These are some critical questions you must answer before writing anything down in your plan of action.

Consider every possibility and prepare yourself for any unexpected setbacks. Setbacks usually come with every plan. Be prepared to sit down, reconsider and rework your strategy. You might even find setbacks to be useful because you will now be able to see the weaknesses in your initial plan and you will be able to come back stronger and more prepared. A setback is simply a setup for a comeback. Don't be discour-aged in your strategies use all your successes and your failures to your advantage.

Sacrifice: As you work towards your deadline what will you have to give up in order to make everything a success? You may find that in order for you to maximize your time and energy you will have to let some things go for a certain time in order to really move forward. This doesn't mean that you can never implement whatever you've sacrificed back into your life. Ingrain this into your mindset *"by any means necessary"*. Channel this statement positively as motivation to have a desire to let things go. Long-term happiness may cost short term sacrifice. It is up to you to decide if it is worth it or not.

Accountability: Who will hold you accountable to see that you meet your deadlines? Will it be a friend, family member, life coach? Whoever you think is best should assist you with your achievements. It is important to have somebody hold you account-able to your commitments. Not everyone needs to know what you are trying to accomplish, however you need someone in your corner rooting for your success and helping you through your setbacks. There is power in unity. Great people always have other great people in there corner because they understand iron sharpens iron. I hope you grasp this and use it to your advantage.

Responsibility: As much as you will have someone to hold you account-able, how will you take responsibility for your actions? This is your goal, your ship and ultimately your life. How will you make sure that you meet your deadline? Maybe you can discuss with your accountability partner what the consequences of failed actions should result in, but this is really all about you. You're the source of power to make this all work. How will you make sure that you stay connected?

Deadline: Depending on the type of goal you have will determine the deadline you set. For example, if this is just a goal you have for the week ask yourself if there are deadlines within the week that you have to meet in order to reach your finish line. Depending on the size of your goal you should create mini deadlines as check points along the way. This will help you to stay focused and stay accurate in wake that you may need to readjust yourself. Make these deadlines realistic because it is up to you to fulfil them. Don't just write down dates, factor in everything that you have to do and then make a decision based off of that. As much as you want to give yourself enough time, you should make sure that you setup your deadlines in a way that keeps you working hard. You don't want to space them out too much because that may lead to complacency and procrastination.

Completion/Reward: How will you reward yourself after each deadline is met? I believe rewards keep us inspired, happy and always allow us to be reminded of our progress. You deserve to be celebrated at every mile-stone whether big or small. Don't wait to be celebrated by other people you know how hard you work and you know how much this means to you. That should be enough for you to give yourself a high five.

TAKE MY ADVICE

REASSES YOUR CIRCLE: There will be individuals in your life that would rather see you fail than see you enjoy the fruit of your labor. Discouragement can come in many different ways and whether it is through a lack of support or even expressed verbally it is important that you never allow it to be a focus. People will say what they want to say and do as they please. That truly has nothing to do with you and ev-erything to do with them. When you see someone discouraging you or not choosing to help you when they can, it should just be a clear indication that they are not for you. Don't let that frustrate you because as much as we would love everyone to love us the reality is not everyone will. Some people will dislike you just because you are you and that's not your fault. I like to look at my haters as my secret admirers because for you to hate me for trying to be progressive, I must be a role model to you. Surround yourself with positive thinking people and constantly tell yourself positive things. I would rather have one loyal person on my team that is for me than ten people that only choose to be there because they have potential gain. It may take you some time to analyze the people in your life and make the right decisions as to who you want in your circle but it is more beneficial to you when you build your support and foundation the right way even if it takes you a little more time than you thought it would. Do it right or don't do it at all. Just because people discourage you doesn't mean you have to allow there discouragement to defeat you.

STEP OUTSIDE YOUR COMFORT ZONE:

Have you ever asked yourself why whatever you are doing hasn't worked out yet? Stepping outside of your comfort zone allows you to be vulnerable and that is something that most people do not like naturally doing. When you step outside of your comfort zone you are immediately allowing yourself to go through a new set of challenges which will give you a new opportunity to grow as a person. Yes it is un-comfortable and frustrating because you are now learning to think and operate in a new way but at the same time the feelings of frustration can be a healthy thing.

If you are learning to do something new or challenging yourself to do something in a new way of course you may get frustrated. The more you learn, the more you get frustrated because the new challenge becomes applicable to what you know. Before musicians are out-wardly great they are inwardly great. They hear the most amazing ideas in their head but the challenge is taking what is in their mind and ap-plying it to their instrument. The process of transferring their ideas to their instrument can be a frustrating one but isn't it not healthy? The end result is they become better at what they do and that growth leads to new opportunities but just like a diamond if you are not willing to go through the fire you cannot be perfected. Trying again doesn't nec-essarily mean trying the same method over again, but instead strategiz-ing and retrying in a different way. If you stay in your comfort zone you will get all that your comfort zone has to offer and that is everything you currently have.

STAY CALM AND GIVE YOURSELF TIME:

There may be a fork in the road but that doesn't mean there cannot be another way. It is ok to be innovative just be authentic to you. If there is a fork in the road and there seems to be no other way learn to blaze a new trail.

Every pathway to success that you see today had to be paved by some-one. Some pathways are quick and others aren't as ideal but nonetheless they are simply just pre-paved roads for onlookers to use in their quest.

It may just be that you weren't built to travel on some of those roads.

Don't expect yourself to get it right on the first try. It is okay to make mis-takes just know that after all your failed attempts you will definitively have something that is proven and workable. Timing is everything and it is not only about getting to the destination, but also the growth and experience that comes along with it. How you choose to act throughout your journey will only highlight the true nature of your character. Always keep the big picture in mind.

TAKE ACTION AND DON'T PLAY THE BLAME GAME: In life things do not just magically happen. There is always an action that causes a reaction. Your purpose will not be fulfilled by you just dwelling all day and night. The difference between a *boss mentality* and a *boss status* is thought vs action. When your thoughts become actions it changes from just a mentality to both a mentality and status. For you to take action, you need to have a plan in place. How are you going to make it happen? What steps are you going to take? What is first? What is priority?

These are all questions that will help you develop your strategy because a plan without a strategy is ineffective. The longer you blame people and things for your inability to progress will be the more the blame will be on you. As long as you play the blame game you will always be a slave to the person you are blaming. There has to be a point where you have to just get over whatever it is and move forward. You cannot live your life waiting for an apology because sometimes it may just never come. It is not worth staying stagnant because of a person or situation when you have the power to move forward. Don't expect the world from those who cannot even provide the world for themselves.

"Your purpose will not be fulfilled by just dwelling all day and night. The difference between a *boss mentality* and a *boss status* is thought vs action."

MY FINAL THOUGHTS

Science teaches us that water is pure and anything that is added to it will change its scientific equation. Water is also literal life. 70-75% of our body is made up of water. I want you to think about this for a moment. You are your own scientific equation. You cannot be duplicated and you cannot be modified. You are original, pure and the life and dreams God has given you are not outside of you but rather inside of you. This means that it is a part of the makeup of your equation. People may have similar tools and pieces but they will never have the same equation as you.

THEIR FORMULA CANNOT CREATE THE DREAM GOD HAS GIVEN YOU.

This means no matter what has already been created and no matter how successful it is, the world is waiting for your dream to show up. You have something that has never been introduced to the world before and you have the power to demonstrate these talents.

NO ONE CAN STEAL YOUR SUCCESS BECAUSE

NO ONE CAN STEAL YOUR EQUATION.

It's time that you fearlessly move forward knowing that God will never give you a dream that wasn't already a finished product. It is just your job to introduce that dream to the world. The dream is alive because you are!

DREAMS ARE FREE.

Your thoughts of fulfillment and abundance are yours regardless of your circumstances and only you have the power to really make things happen. People can try and dictate your physical status to you, however no one can truly determine your mental and emotional status except you. The problem is never truly the problem, it is your mindset towards the problem that is the issue. Your circumstances may be telling you that your dream is never meant to come to life. Family, friends, coworkers and even finances will try to tell you who you are, but they should not be the dictating factor. Everyone and everything has a voice and you will just have to de-cide which voice you want to listen to. Your dreams are telling you that life can be so much more fulfilling and rewarding if you strive towards them. You need to strive towards becoming the greatest version of yourself in order to truly see that dreams are realities! The more you build yourself, the more your dreams will become achievable. It is time to build and master your best you!

www.ingramcontent.com/pod-product-compliance
Lightning Source LLC
Chambersburg PA
CBHW070107100426
42743CB00012B/2678